A Picture Book of
Robert E. Lee

David A. Adler

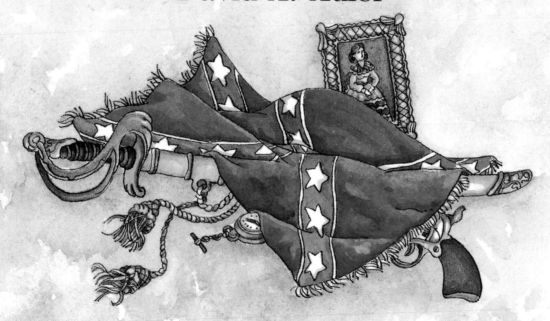

illustrated by John & Alexandra Wallner

Holiday House/New York

Other books in David A. Adler's *Picture Book Biography* series

For Bobby Lasson
D.A.

For Rob Lehmann—
another Southern gentleman
A.W. & J.W.

Text copyright © 1994 by David A. Adler
Illustrations copyright © 1994 by John and Alexandra Wallner
ALL RIGHTS RESERVED
Printed in the United States of America

Library of Congress Cataloging-in-Publication Data
Adler, David A.
A picture book of Robert E. Lee / David A. Adler : illustrated by
John & Alexandra Wallner. —1st ed.
p.   cm.—(Picture book biography)
ISBN 0-8234-1111-7
1. Lee, Robert E. (Robert Edward), 1807–1870—Juvenile literature.
2. Generals—Confederate States of America—Biography—Juvenile
literature. 3. Generals—United States—Biography—Juvenile
literature. 4. Confederate States of America. Army—Biography—
Juvenile literature. 5. United States. Army—Biography—Juvenile
literature. [1. An introduction to the life of the Commander in
Chief of the Confederate Army during the Civil War. 2. Lee, Robert
E. (Robert Edward), 1807–1870. 3. Generals.] I. Wallner, John C.,
ill. II. Wallner, Alexandra, ill. III. Title. IV. Series: Adler,
David A.   Picture book biography.
E467.L4A23   1994   93-22998   CIP   AC
973.7'3'092—dc20
[B]
ISBN 0-8234-1366-7 (pbk.)

Robert Edward Lee was born on January 19, 1807 in Stratford, a large house in Westmoreland County, Virginia. His father was Henry "Light-Horse Harry" Lee, a hero in the Revolutionary War and governor of Virginia. His mother was Ann Hill Carter Lee. Robert was one of five children. Light-Horse Harry had other children, too, from an earlier marriage.

Robert's father lost large sums of money in bad land deals. In 1807, when Robert was born, the grounds outside Stratford were untended. Much of the family's furniture had been sold. In 1809 Light-Horse Harry was so hopelessly in debt that he was locked in the Westmoreland County jail. When he was released one year later, Stratford no longer belonged to him. He and his children moved into a much smaller rented house in Alexandria, Virginia.

In 1812 Henry Lee was injured. He sailed the next year to the British West Indies to regain his health.

Robert was just six years old when his father left. In a letter home, Light-Horse Harry described Robert as "always good," and he was sure the young boy would remain happy in the care of his "ever watchful and affectionate mother."

Henry Lee traveled home in 1818, but he died before he reached Virginia.

Robert's mother was sickly, his father was gone, and his brothers and sisters were either away or too young to help around the house. So Robert cared for his mother, bought food, and tended the yard and horses.

Robert studied, too. One teacher described him as neat, never behind in his work, "a most exemplary student in every respect."

In 1825, Robert left home to begin his career as a soldier. He entered the United States Military Academy at West Point. Before he left, his mother said, "How can I live without Robert? He is both son and daughter to me."

Robert's favorite subject at West Point was engineering, but he did well in all his classes. He graduated second in a class of eighty-seven and was made a lieutenant in the United States Army.

Robert came home in 1829 to find his mother very ill. He stayed with her through the next few weeks until she died.

Lieutenant Lee was assigned to Fort Pulaski, near Savannah, Georgia. He took along Nat, his mother's slave and coachman. Nat was ill, and Robert thought the warm Georgia weather would be good for him. Robert cared for Nat until he died almost a year later.

In 1831 Lee was sent to Fort Monroe in Virginia, close to the home of Mary Anne Randolph Custis, a distant cousin. Robert had known her since they were children. Mary was the great-granddaughter of Martha Washington. Now they were in love. On June 30, 1831, in the Custis family home in Arlington, Virginia, they married.

It was a happy marriage, although Robert's army service kept him away from home for long periods of time. Robert and Mary had seven children: Custis, Mary, William, Annie, Agnes, Robert Edward, Jr., and Mildred.

In 1837 Robert was sent by the army to St. Louis, Missouri, where he built a dike in the Mississippi River to keep the city from flooding. Next he went to New York City where he was in charge of the repair of forts that guarded the harbor. Then, in 1846, the United States declared war on Mexico. Robert was sent to San Antonio, Texas, and then into Mexico.

Robert E. Lee worked as a scout, exploring enemy territory to get information. He also directed the building of bridges that could support heavy army guns being dragged into battle. In the Battle of Veracruz, he helped plan some of the fighting. He was in the thick of the battles for Cerro Gordo and Mexico City. At one point, he was on his horse, riding and fighting, for thirty-six straight hours.

After the war General Winfield Scott, Commander in Chief of the United States Army, called Lee "the greatest military genius in America."

Robert E. Lee was a great soldier, but he hated war. In a letter home he described the shells fired from army guns as "so beautiful in their flight and so destructive in their fall." And he wrote about the people killed: "It was awful. My heart bled. . . . It was terrible to think of the women and children."

In 1852 Robert E. Lee was named superintendent of the United States Military Academy at West Point. He was considered a firm but kind leader who took a real interest in each cadet.

Lee was made lieutenant colonel in 1855 and sent to the Texas frontier to help protect the settlers from attacks by Native Americans.

During the 1850s, the country was divided over the issue of slavery. Owning slaves was allowed in southern states but not in northern ones. In a speech in 1858 Abraham Lincoln said, "I believe this government cannot endure permanently half slave and half free."

Robert E. Lee was home in Virginia in 1859 when John Brown, a passionate fighter against slavery, attacked an army arsenal in Harpers Ferry, Virginia. Brown had hoped to use the weapons to free slaves. Colonel Lee was sent by the army to Harpers Ferry. He had John Brown and his followers arrested.

In November 1860 Abraham Lincoln was elected president. In December South Carolina voted to leave the Union, to secede from the United States, rather than be led by a man who hated slavery. Other slave states followed and together formed the Confederate States of America.

Robert E. Lee hoped and prayed that there would not be war. He said, "In God alone must be our trust."

But on April 12, 1861, Confederate troops fired on Fort Sumter, a U.S. Government fort in South Carolina. The Civil War began. On April 17 Robert E. Lee's home state of Virginia joined the Confederacy.

The prospects for the southern rebel army were not good. There were eleven states in the Confederacy. Twenty-three remained in the Union. There were more people, soldiers, weapons, factories, and railroads in the northern, Union states, than in the southern Confederacy.

Robert E. Lee felt slavery was evil. He had freed his own slaves. He also felt that the nation must remain united. But still, he was torn between remaining in the Union army or joining the forces of Virginia, his home state.

Lee was recognized in both the North and South as a great soldier. President Lincoln chose him to be field commander of the Union army.

Lee refused the assignment and resigned from the U.S. Army. He was a Virginian and he wrote, "I have not been able to make up my mind to raise my hand against my relatives, my children, my home."

On April 22, 1861, Robert E. Lee was appointed commander of the army of Virginia. Soon after that he was named a general in the Confederate army and an adviser to the president of the Confederacy, Jefferson Davis.

In June 1862 General Lee was placed in charge of saving Richmond, Virginia, the capital of the Confederacy. Union generals preparing to attack expected a quick victory, since they had the larger army.

Instead of waiting to defend the city, Lee led his men in attacks against Union forces. The fighting became known as the Seven Days' Battles. Many Confederate soldiers were killed, but Richmond was saved.

In August 1862 the Confederate army won a great victory at Manassas, Virginia, in the second battle of Bull Run. They won because of the strategy of Lee and the leadership of his trusted general, Thomas J. "Stonewall" Jackson.

Robert E. Lee believed it was better to attack the enemy than be attacked, so in September 1862 he led his men into Maryland, a Union state. Union General George B. McClellan learned of Lee's plans and met Lee's forces on September 17, 1862 at Antietam, Maryland. Both sides lost thousands of lives before General Lee retreated to Virginia.

In May 1863, in Chancellorsville, Virginia, Lee's Confederate troops defeated the Union forces, but Stonewall Jackson was killed.

In June 1863, Lee again led his troops onto Union land, this time into Pennsylvania. At the Battle of Gettysburg, during the first three days of July, more than 40,000 soldiers from both sides were killed, wounded, or taken prisoner. Lee's army, unable to continue fighting, withdrew to Virginia.

The Battle of Gettysburg is considered a turning point in the war. After it was over, Lee no longer had a large enough force to stage a major attack.

During much of the war, Robert E. Lee lived in a tent beside his soldiers and shared his food with them. His men showed great respect, even love, for their general. In 1865 Lee was named General in Chief of the Armies of the Confederate States.

In the war there were many battles and much was lost. Houses, farms, railroads, and cities, mostly in the South, were burned to the ground. More than 600,000 soldiers died. Many were killed in battle, but more than half died of disease.

By April 1865 Lee's troops had almost no food. They were greatly outnumbered. To fight just one more day, Lee wrote later, "would have been at a great sacrifice of life and at its end I did not see how a surrender could have been avoided."

On April 9, 1865, at Appomattox Court House in Virginia, General Lee surrendered his forces to General Ulysses S. Grant, commander of all Union armies.

When Robert E. Lee returned to his men, he told them, "Men, we have fought through the war together. I have done the best I could for you. My heart is too full to say more."

He went home to his family. Robert Jr. wrote later that his father "looked older, grayer, more quiet and reserved. He seemed very tired, and was always glad to talk of any other subject than of the war."

Robert E. Lee tried to set an example to his soldiers and others in the South to accept the loss of the war and get back to work without bitterness.

In October 1865 Robert E. Lee was made president of Washington College in Lexington, Virginia. He died in his home on the college campus on October 12, 1870.

Robert E. Lee was brave, wise, and gentle. He was a great general and a leader of men.

People throughout the country mourned for him. Of his death, the *New York Herald*, a northern newspaper, wrote, "Robert E. Lee was an American . . . dignified . . . the idol of his friends and of his soldiers."

Author's Notes

Robert E. Lee's father was called "Light-Horse Harry" because of the quick horseback raids he led against the British during the Revolutionary War.

Light-Horse Harry Lee was married twice. His first wife, Matilda, was a cousin who inherited Stratford from her grandfather. When she died in 1790, she left the house to her and Light-Horse Harry's son Henry. When he turned twenty-one in 1808, the inheritance was his, and he claimed it in 1810.

Harpers Ferry was part of Virginia in 1859. Today it is part of West Virginia, which became a separate state in 1863.

General Stonewall Jackson once said, "So great is my confidence in Robert E. Lee that I am willing to follow him blindfolded." He also said that if he were asked who should lead in an important battle, "I would say with my dying breath, let it be Robert E. Lee."

Washington College is now called Washington and Lee University.

IMPORTANT DATES

1807	Born on January 19 in Westmoreland County, Virginia.
1818	His father, Henry Lee, died.
1825	Entered the United States Military Academy at West Point.
1829	His mother, Ann Hill Carter Lee, died. Graduated from U.S. Military Academy.
1831	Married Mary Anne Randolph Custis on June 30.
1846–1848	Served in the Mexican War.
1852–1855	Served as superintendent of West Point.
1859	Captured John Brown at Harpers Ferry, Virginia.
1861	Resigned commission and joined Confederate army.
1861–1865	The Civil War was fought.
1865	Named General in Chief of the Armies of the Confederate States in February.
1865	Surrendered his forces to General Ulysses S. Grant at Appomattox Court House, Virginia, on April 9.
1865–1870	Served as president of Washington College.
1870	Died in Lexington, Virginia on October 12.